Two Black Cats at the Museum of Modern Art

(Multi Language – English, French and Spanish)

Written and Illustrated by

Phil Dynan

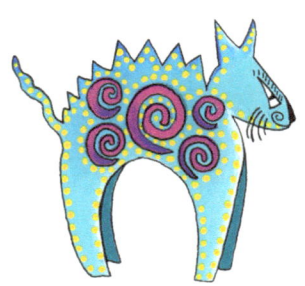

Published by Blue Oaks Arts

P.O. Box 1125, Red Bluff, CA 96080

www.BlueOaksArts.com

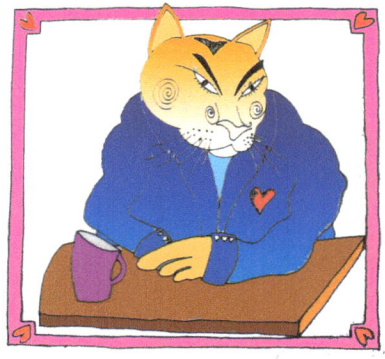

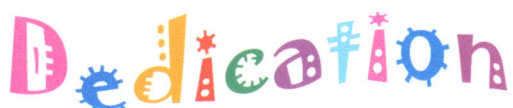

Dedication

Moto & Kozo are two black cats in this book, but they also represent my son and daughter, Joseph and Sara.

The story is based on our trip to London and the events that followed on the day that I "dragged" them to the Museum of Mankind.

Though they had not wanted to visit a "museum", upon their arrival they were given drawing boards and pencils and paper by the Museum staff. They began to draw what they saw in the displays; became friends over lunch with the staff; and found that the art and installations in the Museum were very much "alive" upon closer examination.

Ironically, they refused to leave the Museum until the good-natured staff escorted them to the front door - 30 minutes after closing time!

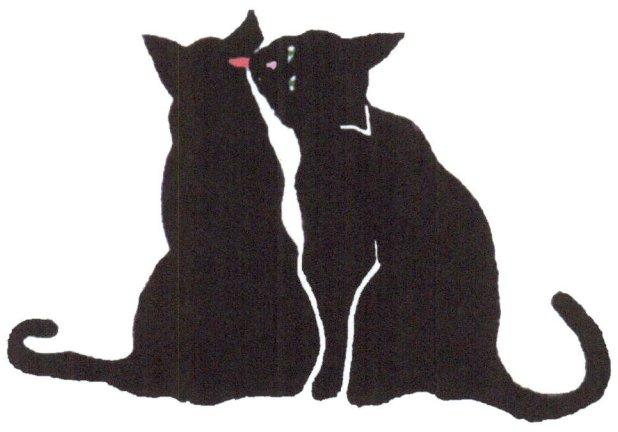

Two Black Cats Visit the Museum of Modern Art (Multi Language – French, English and Spanish)

Written and Illustrated by Phil Dynan

English

Charlie is a docent at the
The Museum of Modern Art. Usually,
Moto and Kozo keep him company
at night. But this evening Kozo
wants Moto to look at the
art in the gallery.

French

Charlie est le conservateur du
"Museum of Modern Art".
Moto et Kozo lui tiennent parfois,
compagnie la nuit.
Mais ce soir Kozo veut que Moto
regarde l'exposition.

Spanish

Charlie es el conservador de "The Museum of Modern Art".
Algunas veces Moto y Kozo lo acompañan en la noche.
Pero ésta noche, Kozo quiere que Moto vea el arte.

Artist's Notes

Working in London over a period of twenty years,
I had often visited the Museum of Mankind to study
cultures and art from exotic places I was not likely to ever
visit.

I thought that Joe and Sara would benefit from a visit
to this extension of the British Museum. But they
weren't interested in "going to a museum".

I had to bribe them to go with the promise of lunch at
McDonalds!

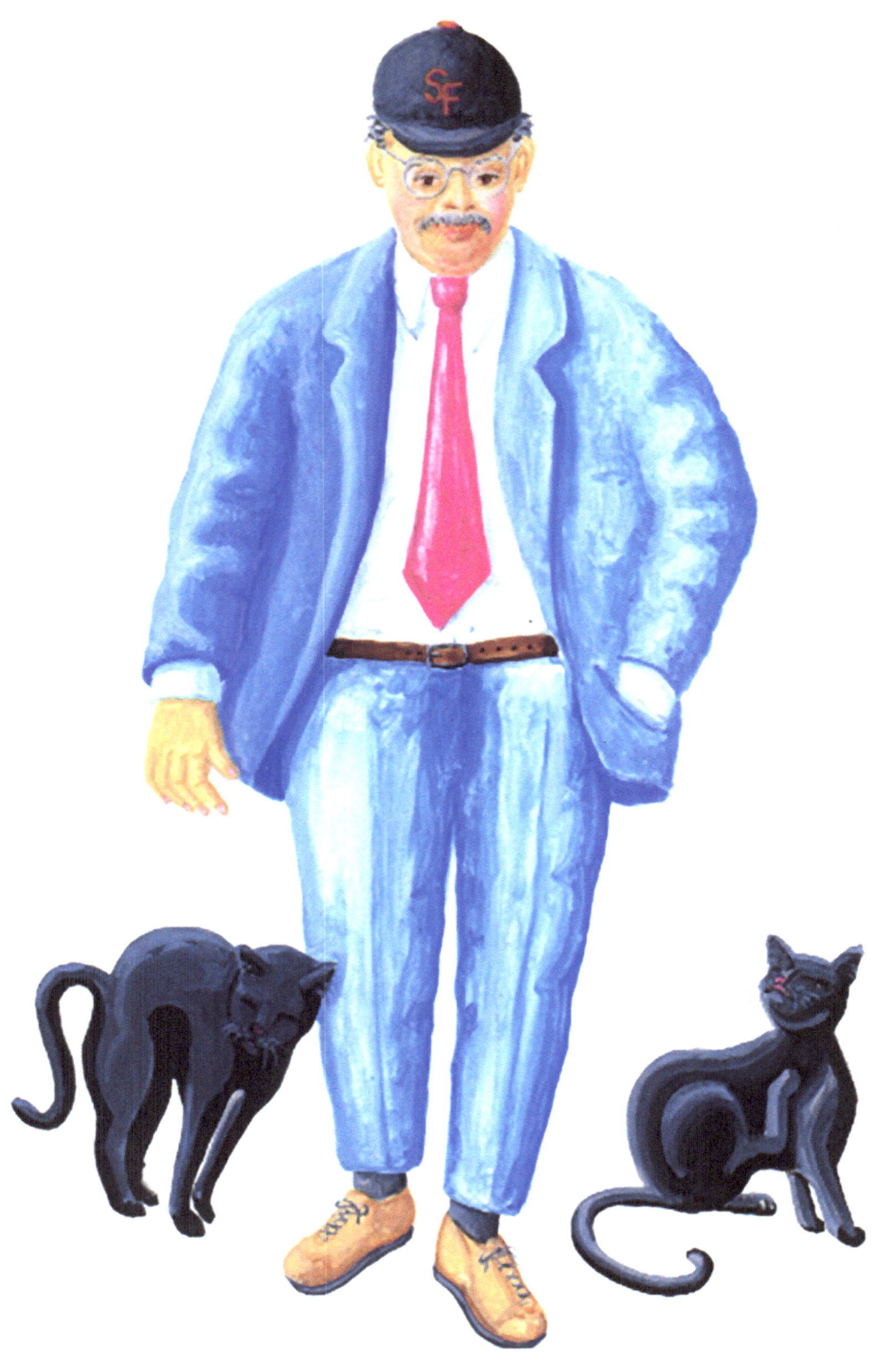

English

"Do we have to look at these pictures?"
asked Moto, "I want to do something more fun."

"Wait and see. You might just
find something interesting in
here." Kozo replied.

French

"Faut-il vraiment que l'on regarde ces tableaux?"
demanda Moto, "J'amerais mieux faire
quelque chose de plus marrant."

"Attends et regarde, tu vas
peut-être trouver quelque
chose d'intéressant ici,"
répondit Kozo.

Spanish

"¿Tenemos que ver estos cuadros?"
pregunta Moto, "Yo quiero hacer
algo más divertido".

"Ya verás. Tal vez encuentres algo
interesante por aquí", responde Kozo.

Artist's Notes

Once we arrived at the Museum, Joe and Sara
immediately started complaining. It is an old
building, and the lobby is very quiet and a little
stuffy.

A docent asked us to take our jackets to the
coat check window in the lobby.

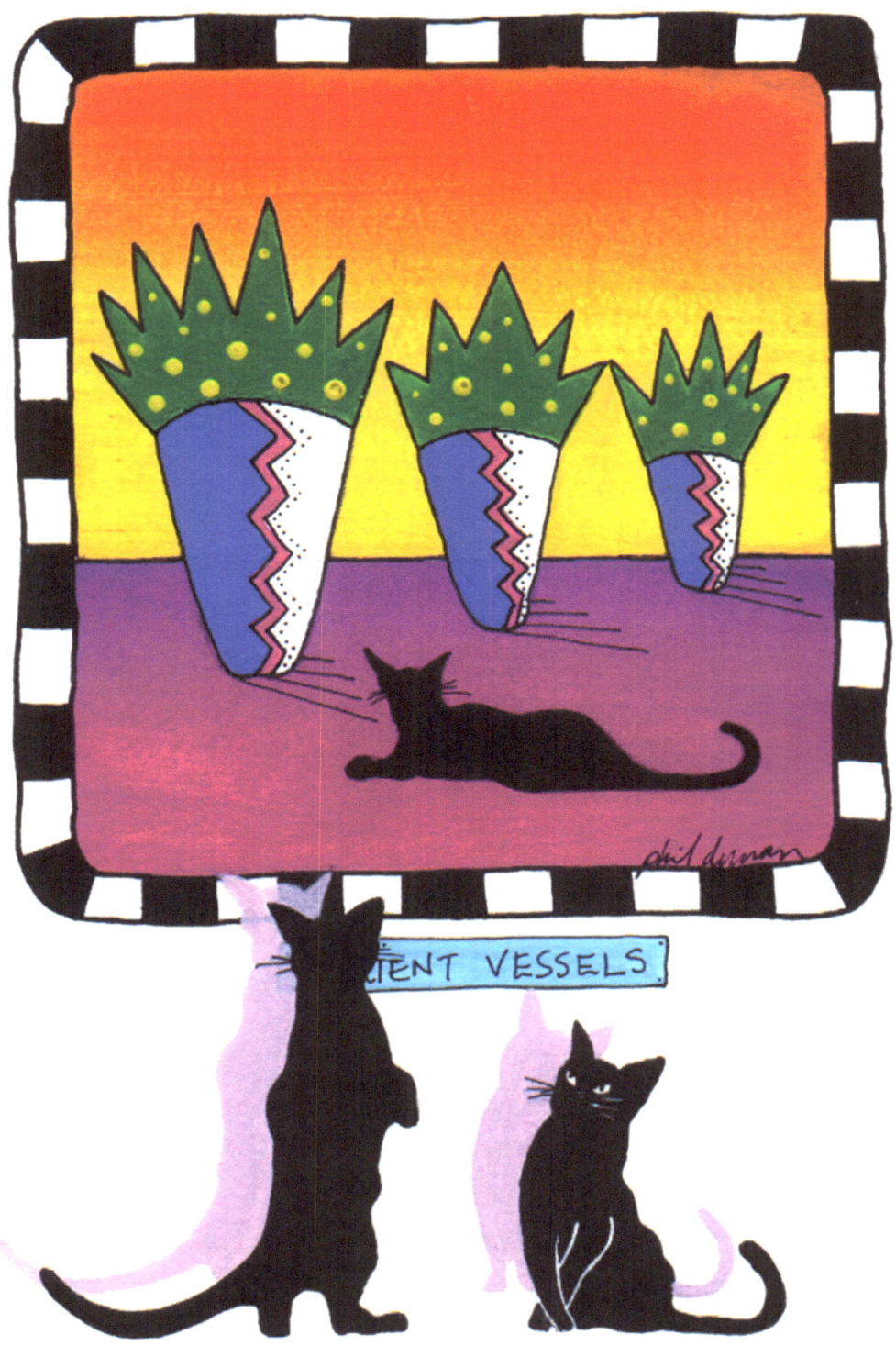

English

"Hey, look, there are things
falling off the picture!"

"Cool." answered Moto.

French

"Tiens, regarde! Il y des
choses qui tombent des
tableaux."

"Super!" répondit Moto.

Spanish

"¡Oye, mira, hay cosas que se estan
cayendo de ese cuadro!"

"Que padré." contesta Moto.

Artist's Notes

The woman at the coat check window could
see quite clearly that the kids were not
entirely happy.

She told them to wait by the window, that
she "had something for them!"

When she returned she gave each of them a large
drawing board, art paper and colour pencils.

Joe and Sara brightened up at this gesture!

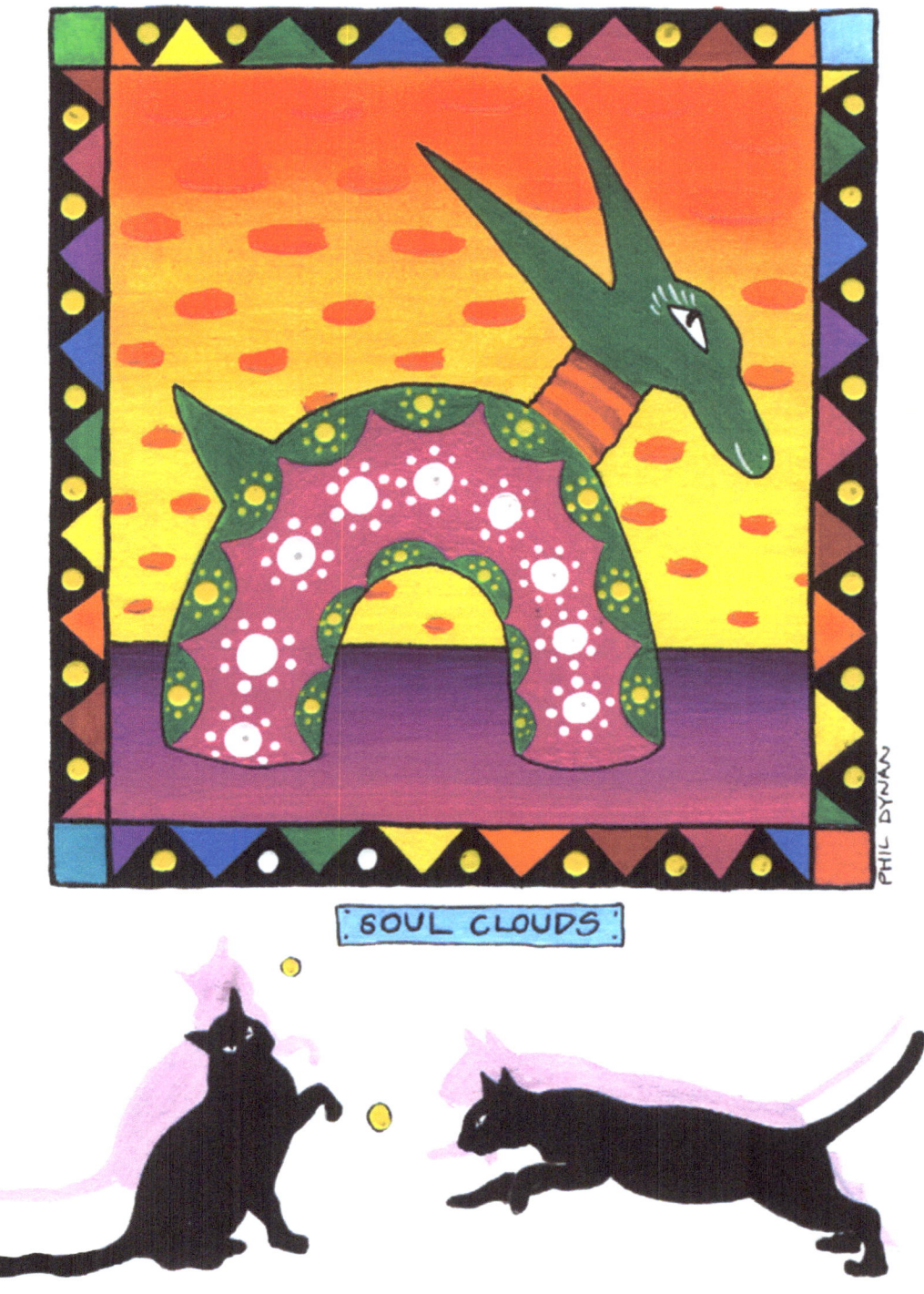

English

"Did you see that, Kozo?"

"What?"

"She moved . . . didn't you see her spin around?"

"Psycho-cat." Kozo muttered
under his tuna-breath.

French

"T'as vu ça, Moto?"

"Quoi?"

"Elle a bougé . . . tu ne l'as pas vu faire une pirouette?"

"Il est bizarre ce chat," marmonne Moto, lachant
un petit rot de son haleine de poisson.

Spanish

"¿Viste eso Kozo?"

"¿Qué?"

"Ella se movió . . . ¿qué no la viste
voltearse?"

"Gato psicópata," murmuro Kozo con
aliento de atún.

Artist's Notes

Now that Joe and Sara were armed with
drawing materials, they started looking for
something to draw.

Their irritation with me for forcing them to
"visit a museum" was disappearing and they
began to take an interest in the displays.

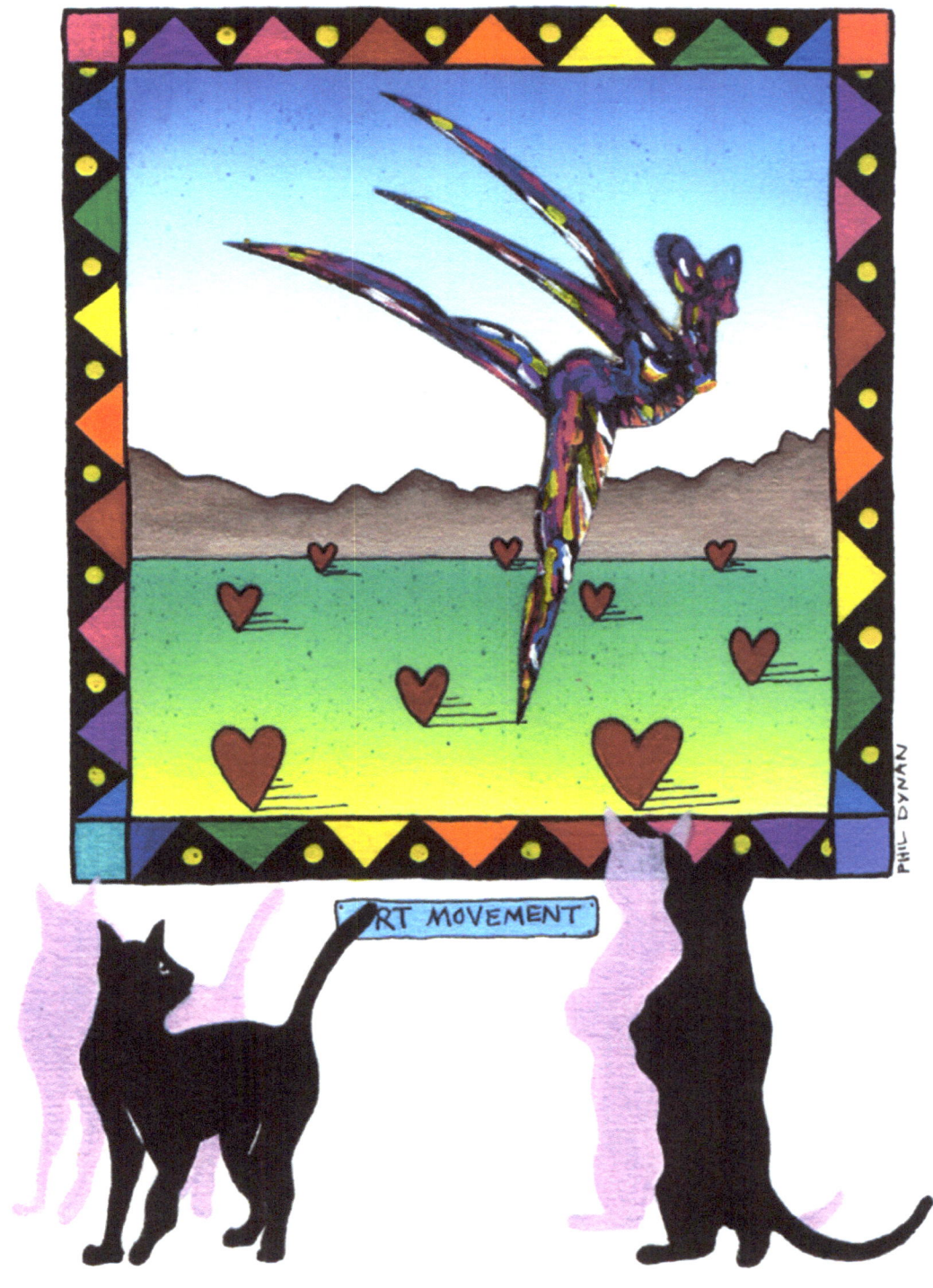

English

"Whoooooaaaa!!!! It's a
flyin' coconut, Man!" Kozo
was electrified.

"Whatever." Moto said..

French

"Wow! Genial! C'est une noix
de coco volant!"
Kozo était surexcité.

"Ouais, ouais," dit Moto.

Spanish

"¡Hiiiiiijole!!! ¡"Es un coco volador!"
Kozo estaba electrificado.

"Así es," dijo Moto.

Artist's Notes

Climbing the stairs to the second floor, Joe and Sara
found an interactive video presentation that
allowed them to explore Iceland.

As they "navigated" a boat along a river that
was surrounded by snow and unfamiliar animals,
they were definately beginning to see
the possibilities in the Museum.

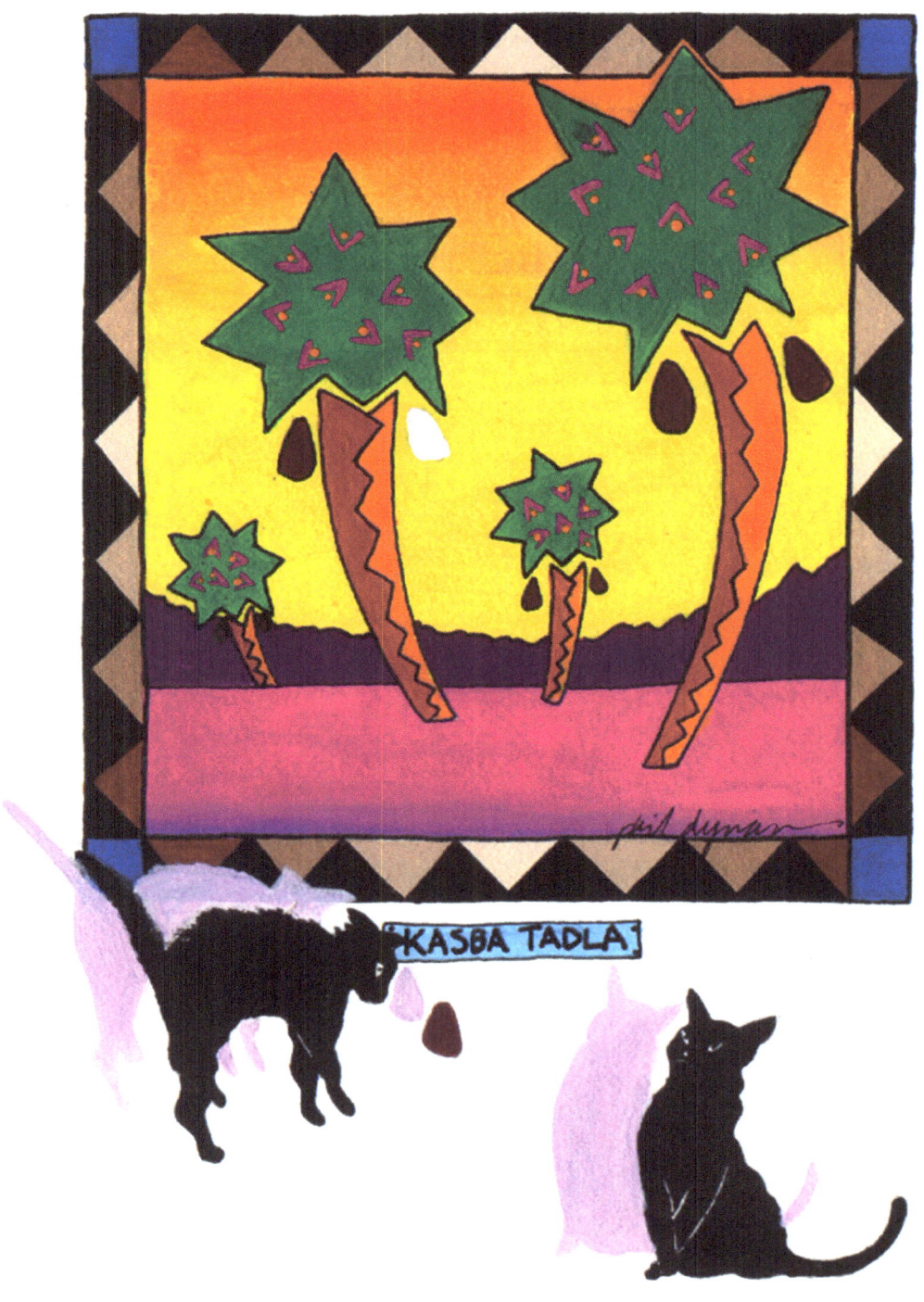

English

"Hey, check this out."

"What? So what?"

"It isn't a ball. It's one of lizard-boy's spots."

"Weird." said Kozo.

French

"Vise un peu ça?"

"Quoi? . . . Et alors?"

"Ce n'est pas une balle, c'est une tâche de lézard."

"C'est bizarre!" dit Kozo.

Spanish

Oye, miro ésto."

"¿Sí, y qué?"

"No es una pelota. Es la mancha del amigo-lagartija."

"Qué raro," dijo Kozo.

Artist's Notes

Joe & Sara were looking at a life-sized reproduction of an African straw dwelling. It was an accurate and complete model, with shields made from metal beer advertising signs.

They were trying to get closer to the life-like models of the family who lived in the hut, when a docent broke the silence of the Museum.

The Museum seemed to be coming to life from every corner!

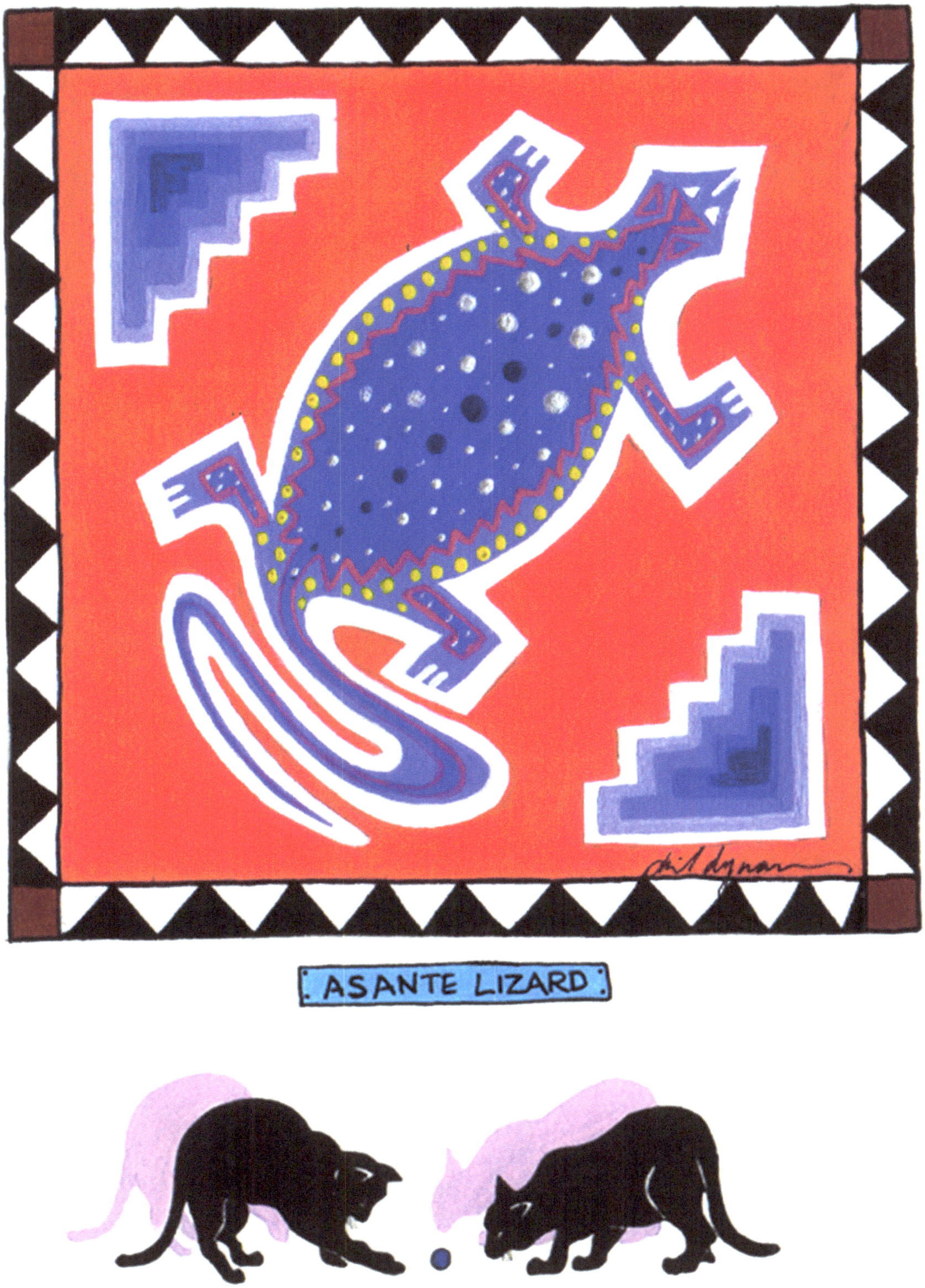

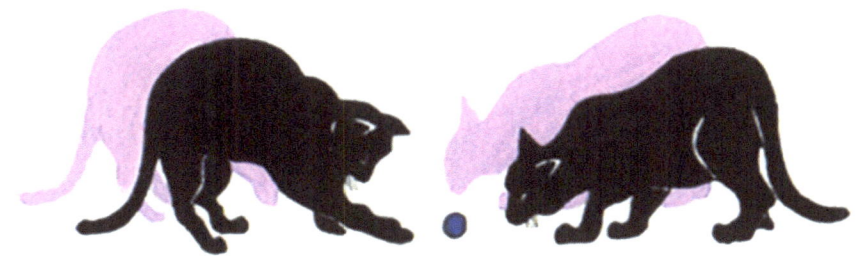

ASANTE LIZARD

English

"What's up with this guy?"

"I think he is looking right at us . . ."

"You think those white snakes are a reference to
Heavy Metal?" Moto mused.

French

"Mais, qu'est-ce qui se passe avec celui-là?"

"Zut! Il nous regarde. . ."

"Tu ne crois pas que ces serpents blancs font partie
de Hard Rock?" chuchota Moto.

Spanish

"¿Qué pasa con éste amigo?"
"Pienso que nos ve directamente . . ."

"¿Piensas que esas serpientes blancas
se refieren al Rock Pesado?" comenta
Moto muy distraído.

Artist's Notes

As we slowly made our way through the Museum, Joe
and Sara both started to interact with the docents
stationed near each display.

They were becoming more and more absorbed in
the Museum.

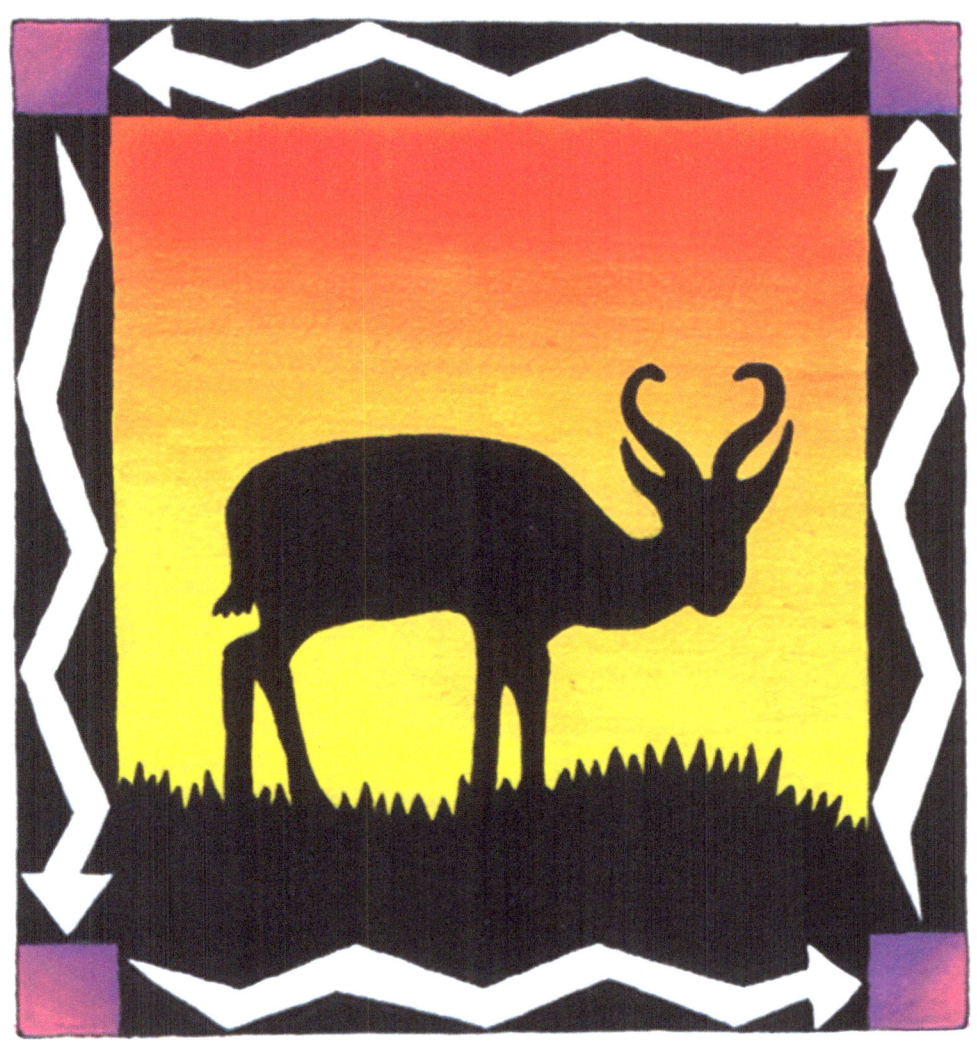

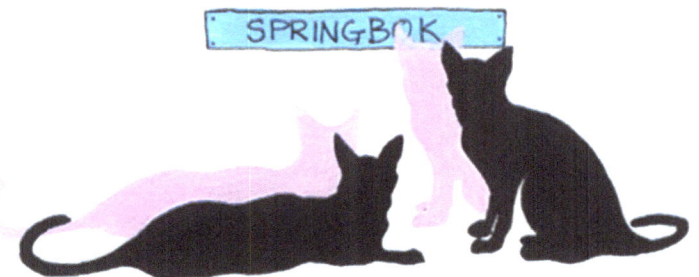

SPRINGBOK

English

"Things falling out of pictures,
animals following us around,
this could be scary!" said
Kozo.

"Hey, maybe I can get
another ball off this canvas."
Moto replied.

French

"Des trucs qui tombent des
tableaux, des animaux qui
nous suivent . . . ça commence à
me faire peur," dit Kozo.

"Tiens, peut-être que je peux
récuperer une autre balle de
ce tableau," repond Moto.

Spanish

"Cosas cayéndose de los cuardros, animales
siguiéndonos, "¡ésto puede ser espantoso!"
dijo Kozo.

Oye, quizás podría sacar otra pelota de la
lona," contesta Moto.

Artist's Notes

Working our way upstairs to the top floor,
I noticed a clock in the hall.

Joe and Sara hadn't noticed, but it
was well into the afternoon. They
had completely forgotten
about McDonalds.

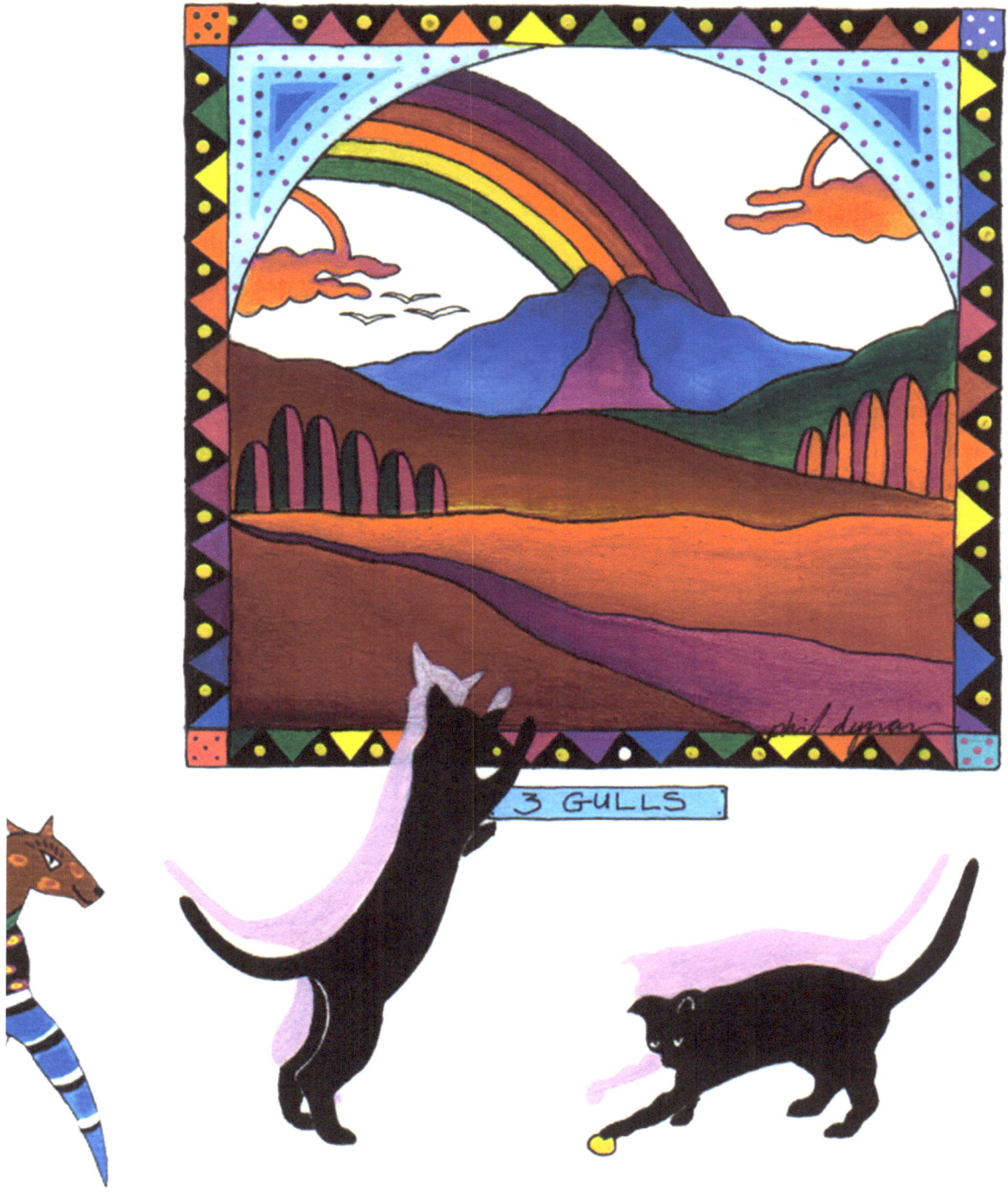

3 GULLS.

English

"Wow, this is great!" Moto was having a good time.

"I don't think Ian is going to like this mess."

"Yeah, well wait til he sees the creatures that are following us!"

French

"WOW! C'est super cool!" dit
Moto qui était en train de s'amuser follement.

"Je ne crois pas que Yann va apprecier ce comportement."

"Tu l'as dit! Et attends quand il va voir toutes ces bêtes qui nous suivent!"

Spanish

"¡Híjuela, qué padre!" Moto se estaba divertiendo.

"Pienso que a Charlie no le gustará éste desorden."

"¡Pues espérate tantito, cuando vea las especies raras que nos siguen!"

Artist's Notes

I asked the kids if they wanted something to eat. Joe and Sara were so busy drawing that they didn't answer at first.

But when they had each finished at the current display they told me they wanted something to eat.

A docent took us down to the tea room and bought them snacks. She called over two other docents. We all had high tea together.

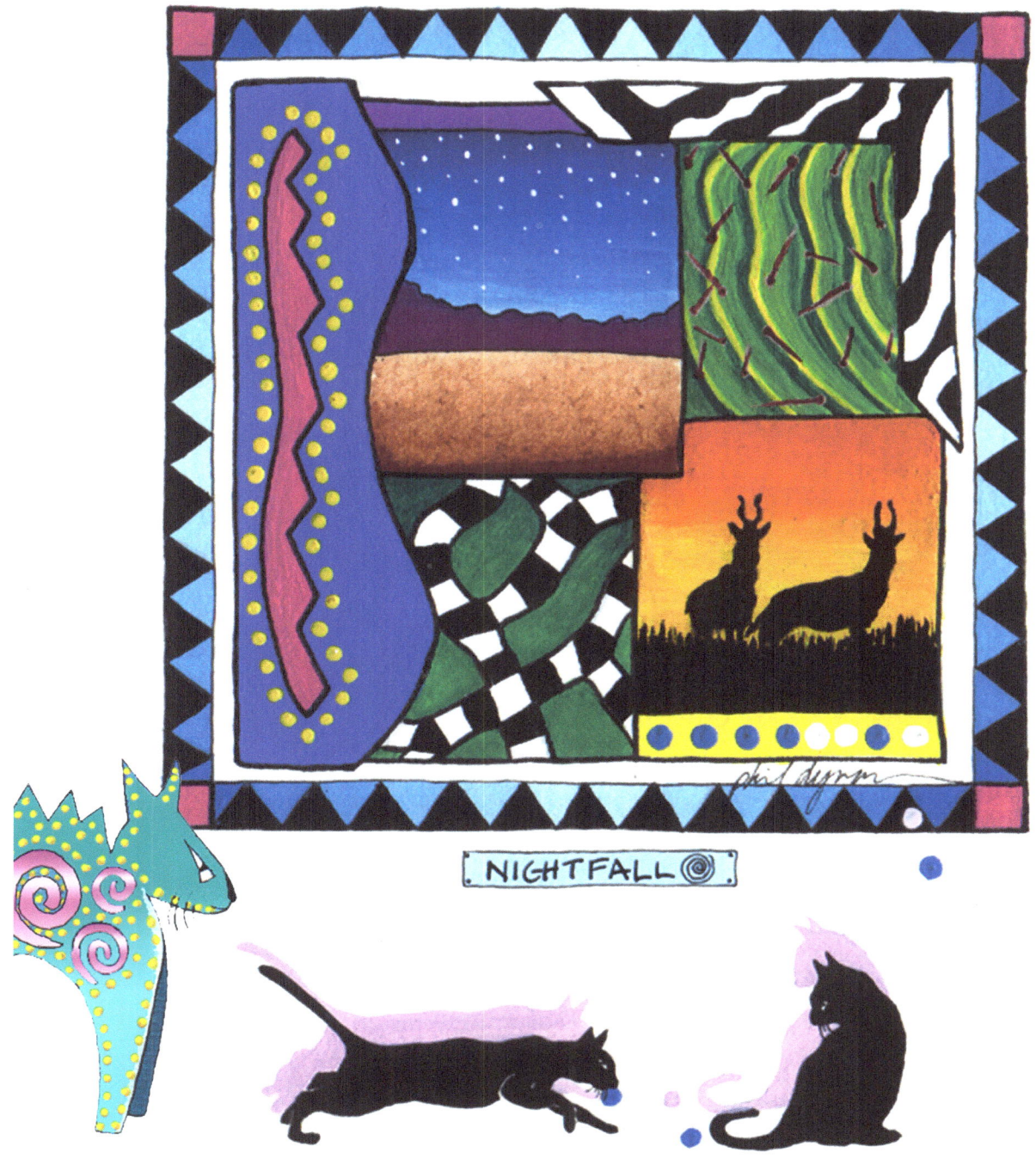

NIGHTFALL

English
"Can you, like, juggle all these balls?" Moto asked Kozo.

"Can you, 'like', just grow up?"

"Whew! Feeling a little hostile?"

French
Comme ça, tu peux jongler avec toutes ces balles?" demande Moto.

"Tu peux grandir un peu!"

"Eh, t'es pas cool!" dit Moto.

Spanish

"¿Puedes lanzar todas éstas pelotas?"
Moto le preguntó a Kozo.

"¿Podrías compórtate con madurez?"

"¡Vaya, ¿estás un poco hóstil?"

Artist's Notes

After tea, Joe and Sara wanted to get back to the displays. We'd already seen everything, but they insisted that they had missed some exhibits.

It was within an hour of closing time and I had the feeling that now I was going to have a difficult time getting the kids to leave the Museum.

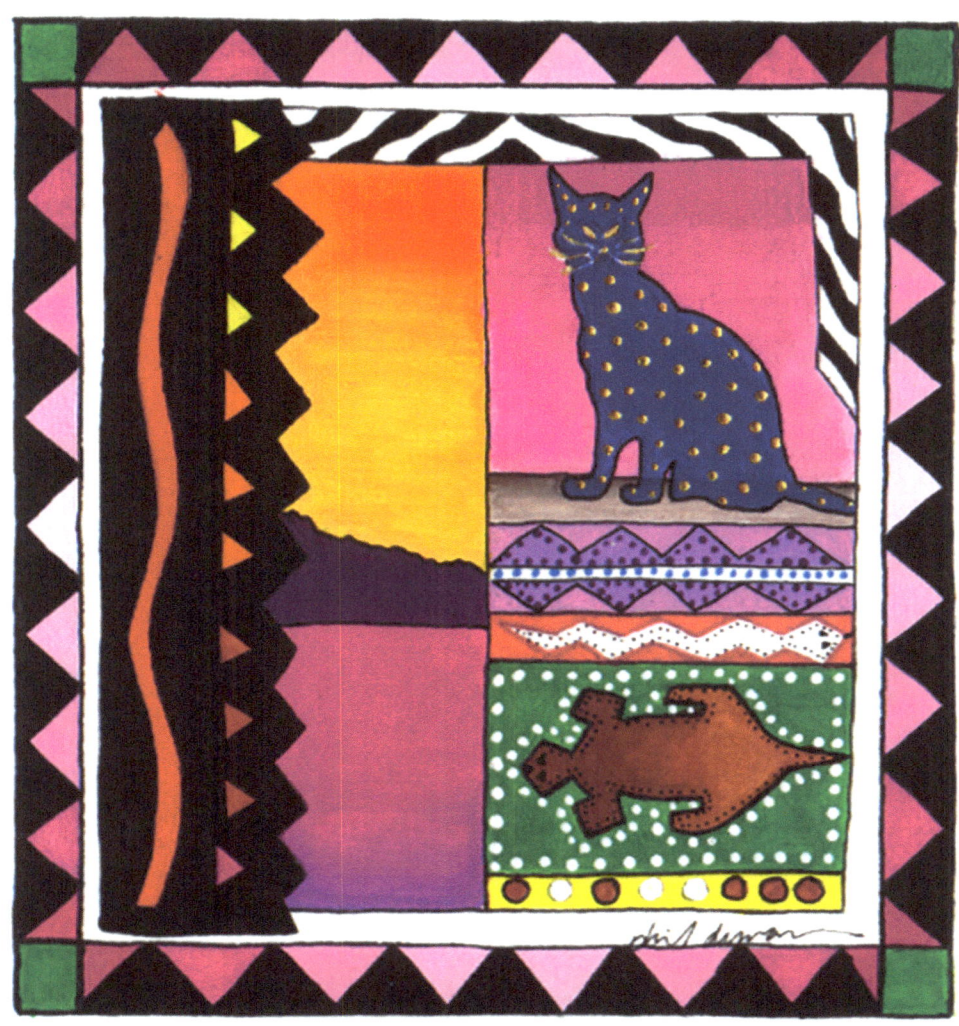

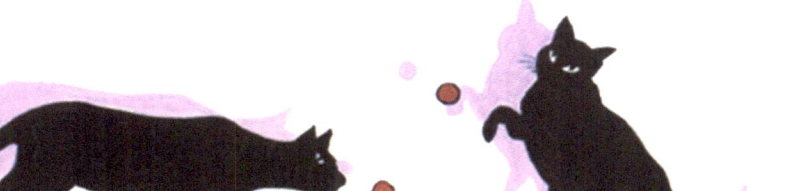

English

"Hey Moto, I've got an idea."

"Yeah, what's up?"

"Why don't you grab that leaf and see if it's real. . ."

"Uhhh, it feels just like a leaf."

French

"J'ai une idée."

"Raconte, vas-y."

"Attrape cette feuille pour voir si elle est vraie."

"C'est vraiment une feuille?"

Spanish

"Oye Moto, tengo una idea."

"¿Sí, qué pasa?"

"Porqué no agarras esa hoja para ver si
es de verdad . . ."

"Uh, se siento como una hoja."

Artist's Notes

Many of the displays in the Museum are life-sized.

Joe and Sara continued to draw and explore, with
almost unlimited people, animals, and objects to
work from.

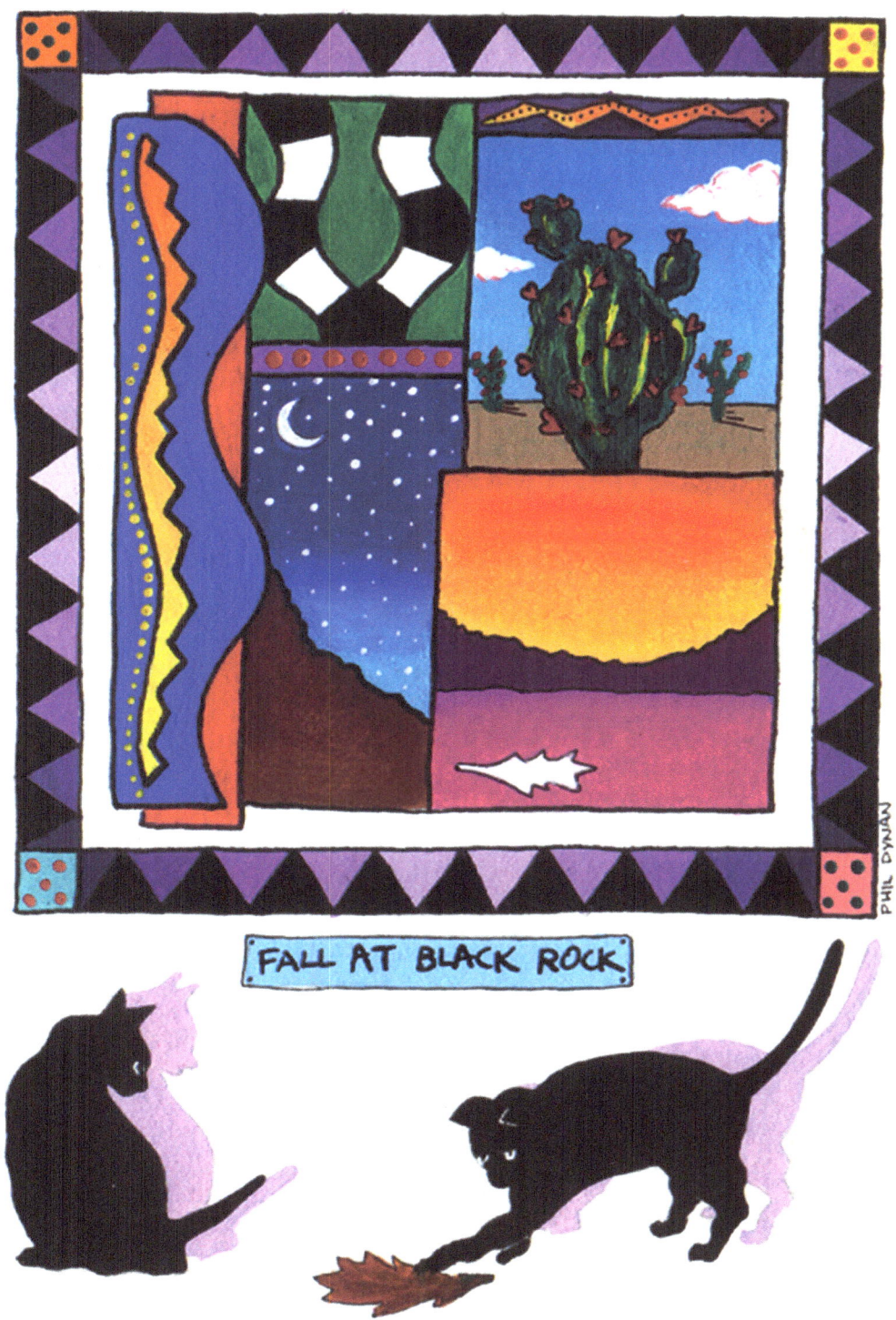

English

"Why do I feel like someone is watching us?"

"I don't know. Why don't you just chill for awhile?"

"OK," Moto said, "right after I get this
cowlick off of you."

French

"Tu sais, J'ai l'impression que
quelqu'un nous observe."

"Je ne sais pas, mais calme-toi pour un instant."

"D'accord, mais laisse-moi te lécher un bon
coup." dit Moto.

Spanish

"¿Porqué siento que alguien nos está mirando?"

"No sé. ¿Porqué no te calmas un poco?"

"Está bién", dijo Moto, "después de que te quite éste remolino."

Artist's Notes

As they worked their way around the Museum, they
befriended the docents and had even managed to
get a dinner invitation from one.

I felt so proud of Joe and Sara. I also had my sketch book
and it was that day in the Museum that I started
drawing out the idea for this book.

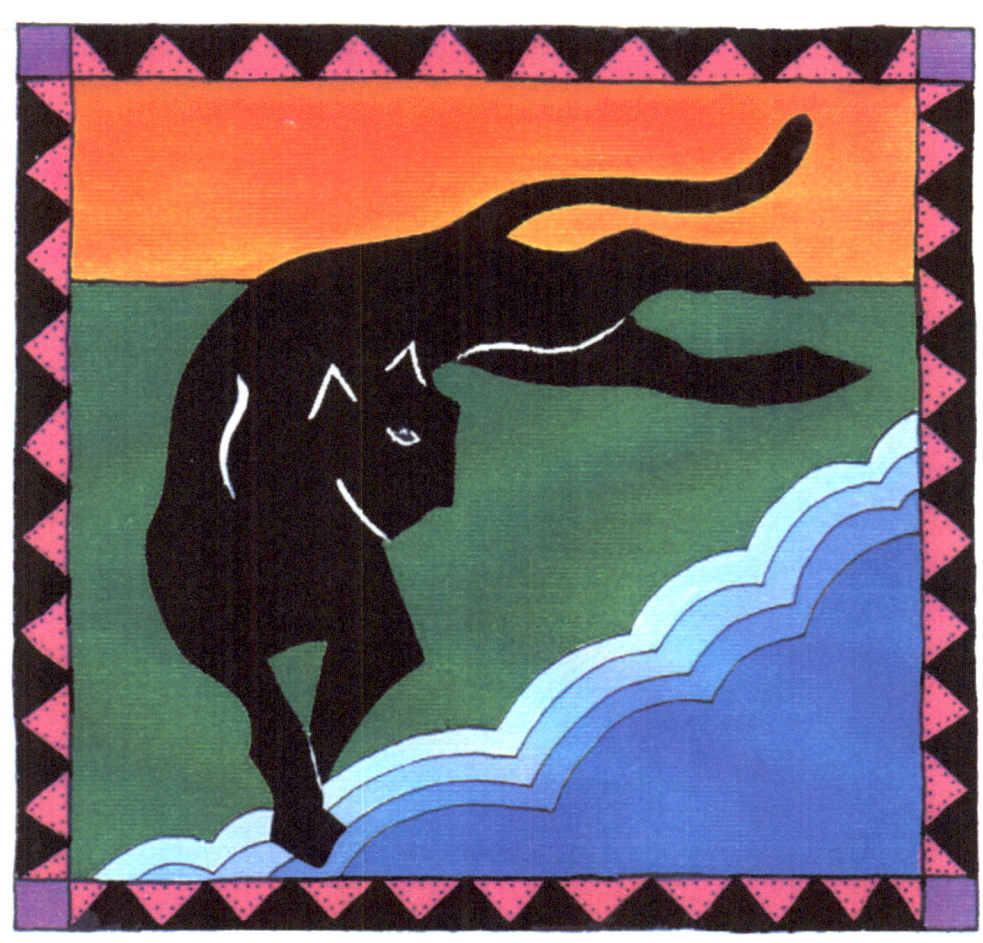

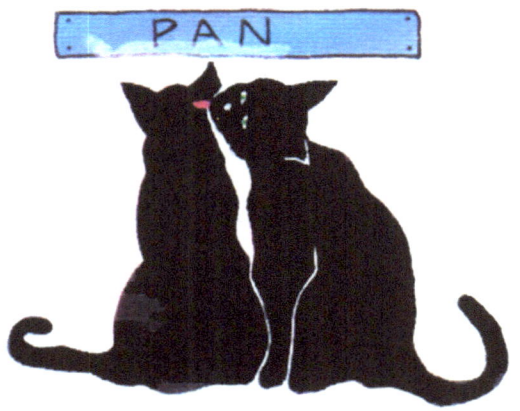

English

"Hey, get this thing off my head!" yelled Moto.

"Well, got your head stuck in the clouds again?"

"This isn't funny. Get it off my head."

French

"Enlève ce machin de sur ma tête," s'écrie Moto.

"Tiens, tiens, Monsieur a encore la tête dans les nuages!"

"Bon ça suffit! Enlève-moi ça de la figure!"

Spanish

"¡Ay, quítame ésto de la cabeza!" gritó Moto.

"Bueno, ¿qué tienes la cabeza en las nubes otra vez?"

"No estés bromeando. Quítemalo de la cabeza."

Artist's Notes

This book has now been published in three languages. It has also been published with all three on one page (like this one). The first tri-language book was made especially for the Davis Bi-lingual school in Tucson, Arizona; but it has now been republished as part of an international literacy campaign.

So, in a way, Joe and Sara have given back to the different cultures that they spent exploring that day in the Museum of Mankind.

Everything is connected. It all comes full-circle.

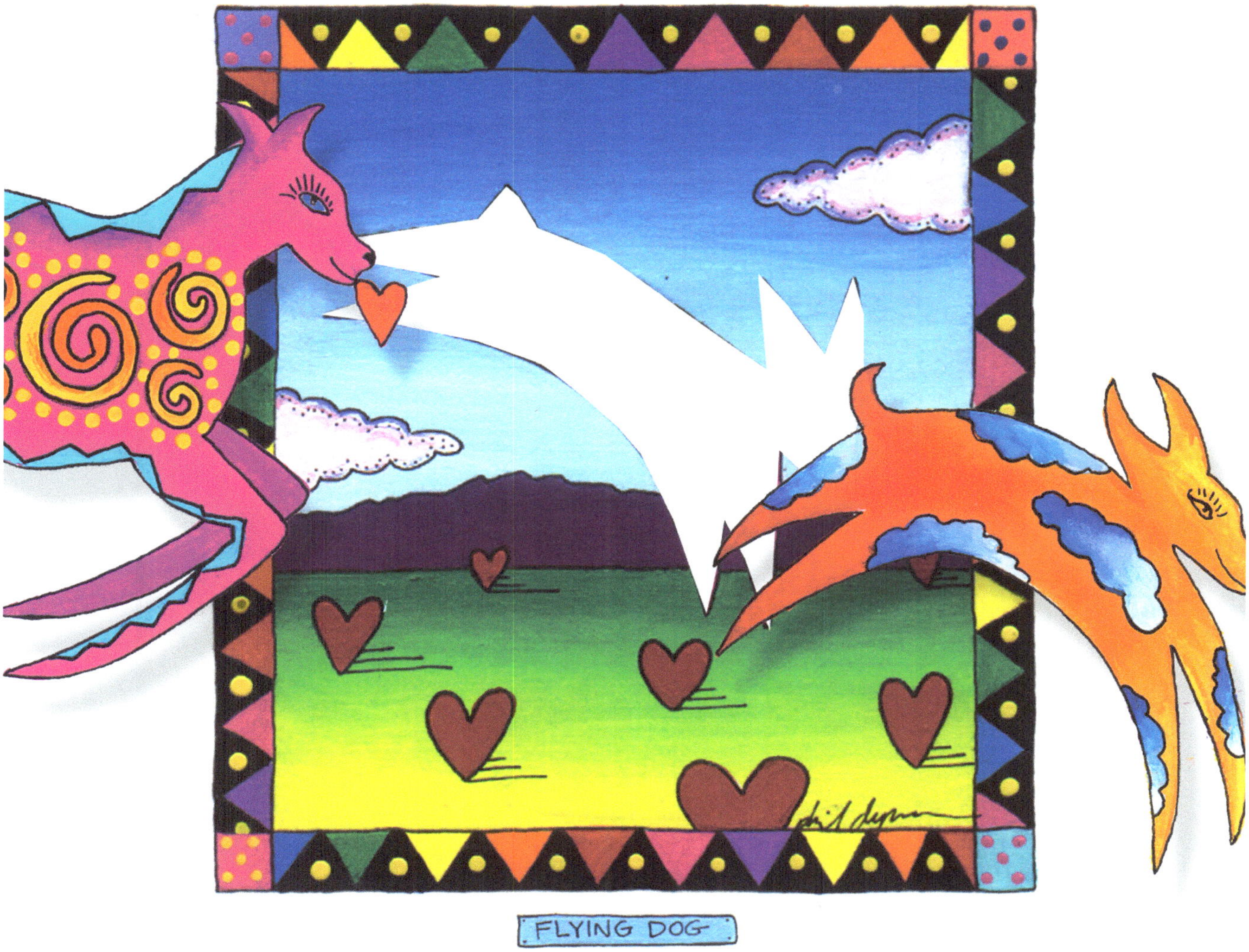

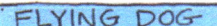

FLYING DOG

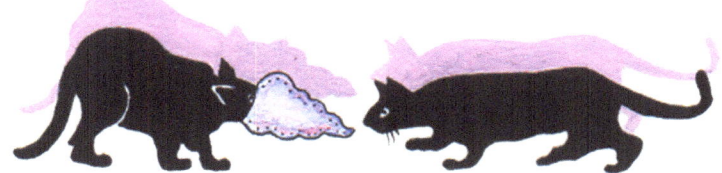

English

"I wonder if I can get this guy to jump
off the picture?"

"Don't move, Moto, I think something is following
you . . . here, I'll just grab it for you."

French

"Je me demande si je peux faire sauter ce
gars-là hors du tableau?"

"Moto ne bouge pas d'un poil! Je crois qu'il y a
quelque chose qui te suit . . . ça y est, Je l'ai!"

Spanish

"Me pregunto, ¿pudiera hacer que éste amigo brinque del cuadro?"

"No te muevas Moto, creo que algo te está siguiendo . . . toma,
yo lo agarraré."

Artist's Notes

Eventually, I painted over 100 pictures featuring Moto and Kozo. Most
of the paintings also had little elements of my own travels hidden in them.
Bits of Eritrea, Ethiopia, France, Greece, Italy, Sweden, Denmark, and Britain. Bits
of things I saw at the British Museum and the Museum of Mankind.

The original version of this book was painted in a handmade book
made of khaddi paper. There are about twice as many illustrations in the
original version.

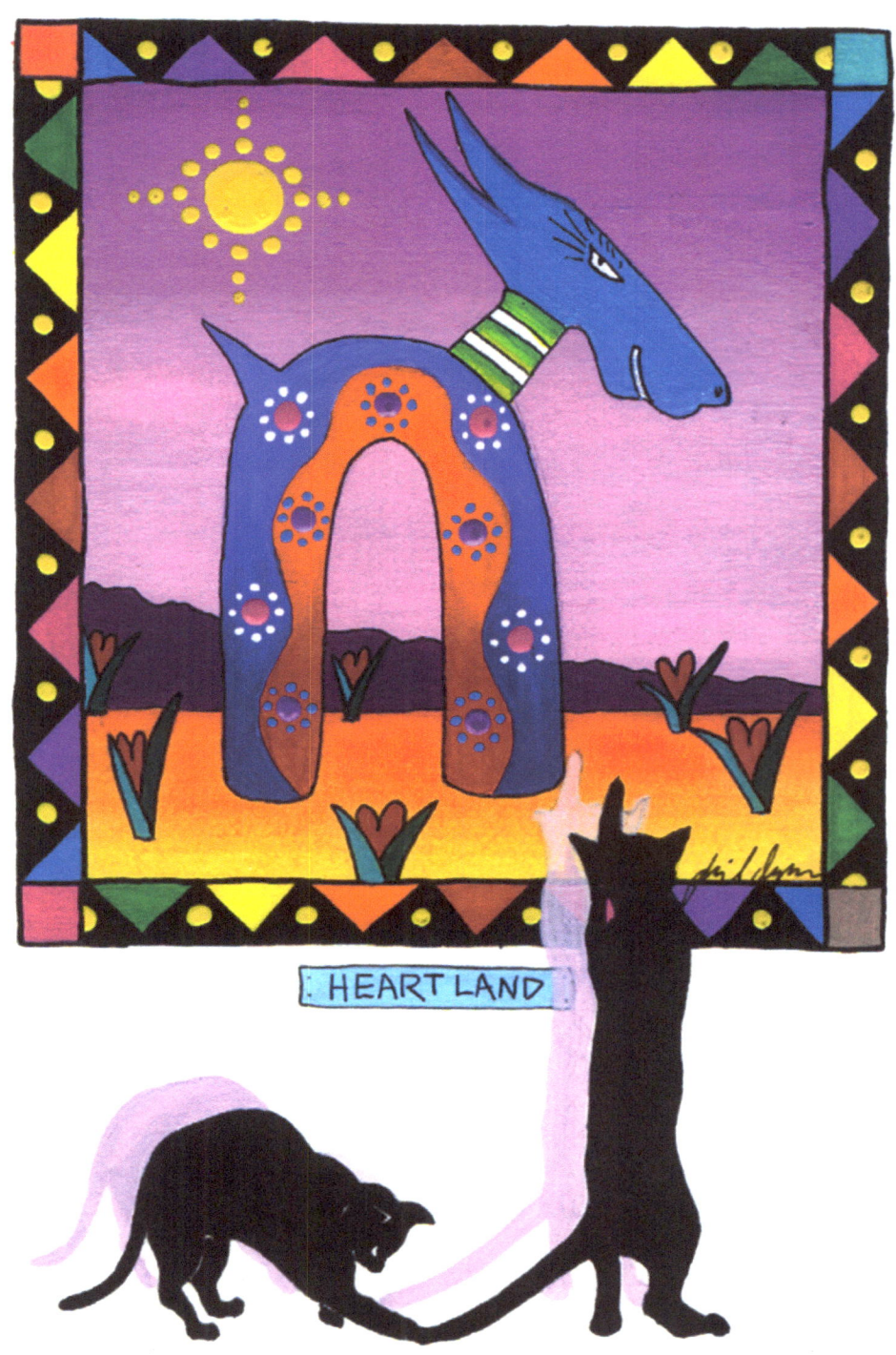

HEART LAND

English

"You know what, Kozo?" Moto said, "This place
isn't so bad after all. A little weird. But pretty cool."

"Yeah, very cool." Kozo said, "Let's go find Charlie."

French

"Tu veux que je te dise quelque chose Kozo? L'endroit
est un peu bizarre, mais trés cool," dit Moto.

"Ouais, super cool!" dit Kozo.

"Allons retrouver Charlie."

Spanish

"¿Sabes qué Kozo? No está tan mal éste lugar. Un poco raro.
Pero a toda dar."

"Claro, qué a todo dar," dijo Kozo, "Vamos a buscar a Charlie."

Artist's Notes

The Museum of Mankind was quite understanding when Joe and Sara weren't
quite done drawing at closing time. The kids were allowed to finish their
drawings and we left about a half hour after closing.

"Going to a museum" had turned out to be pretty cool.

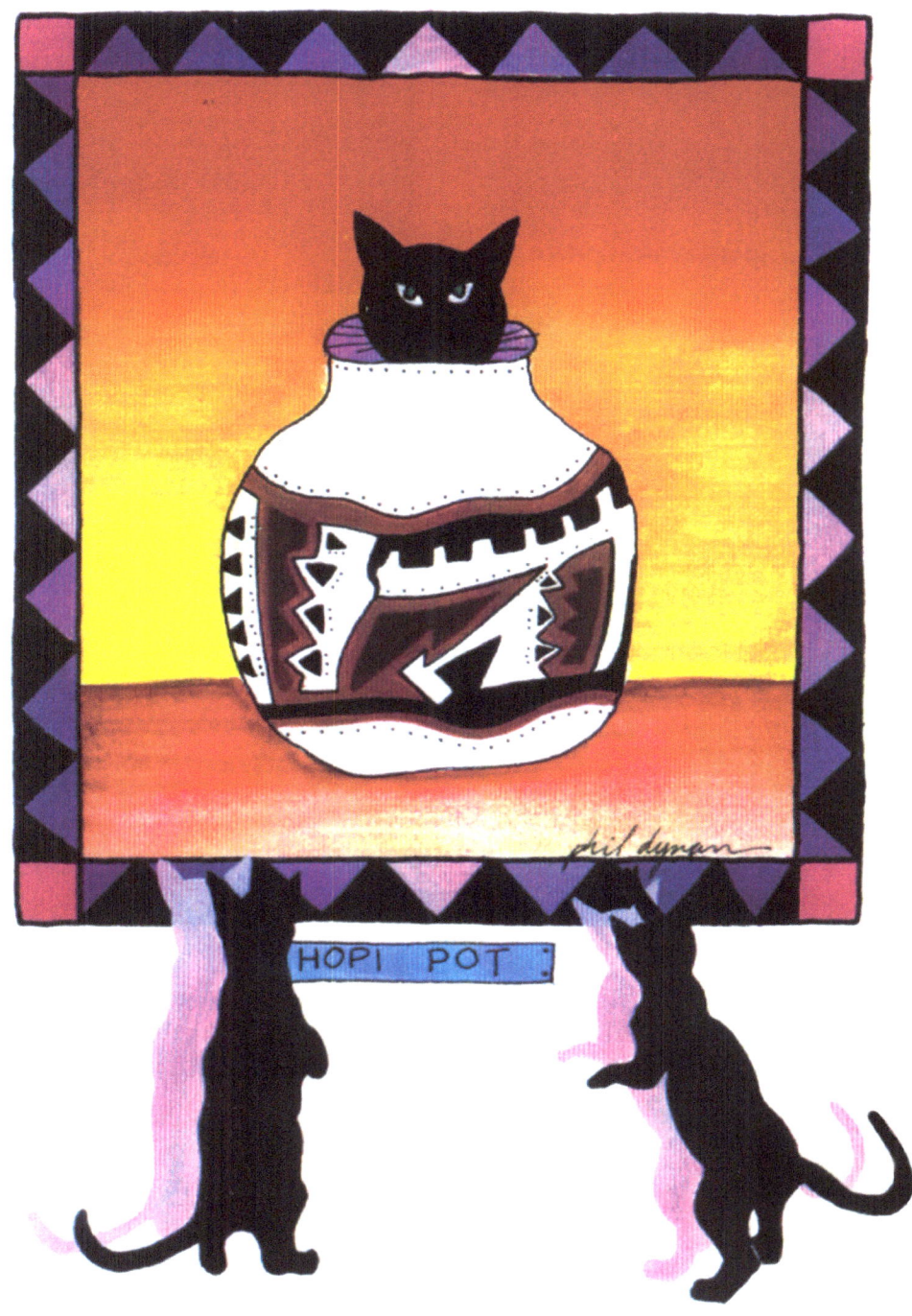

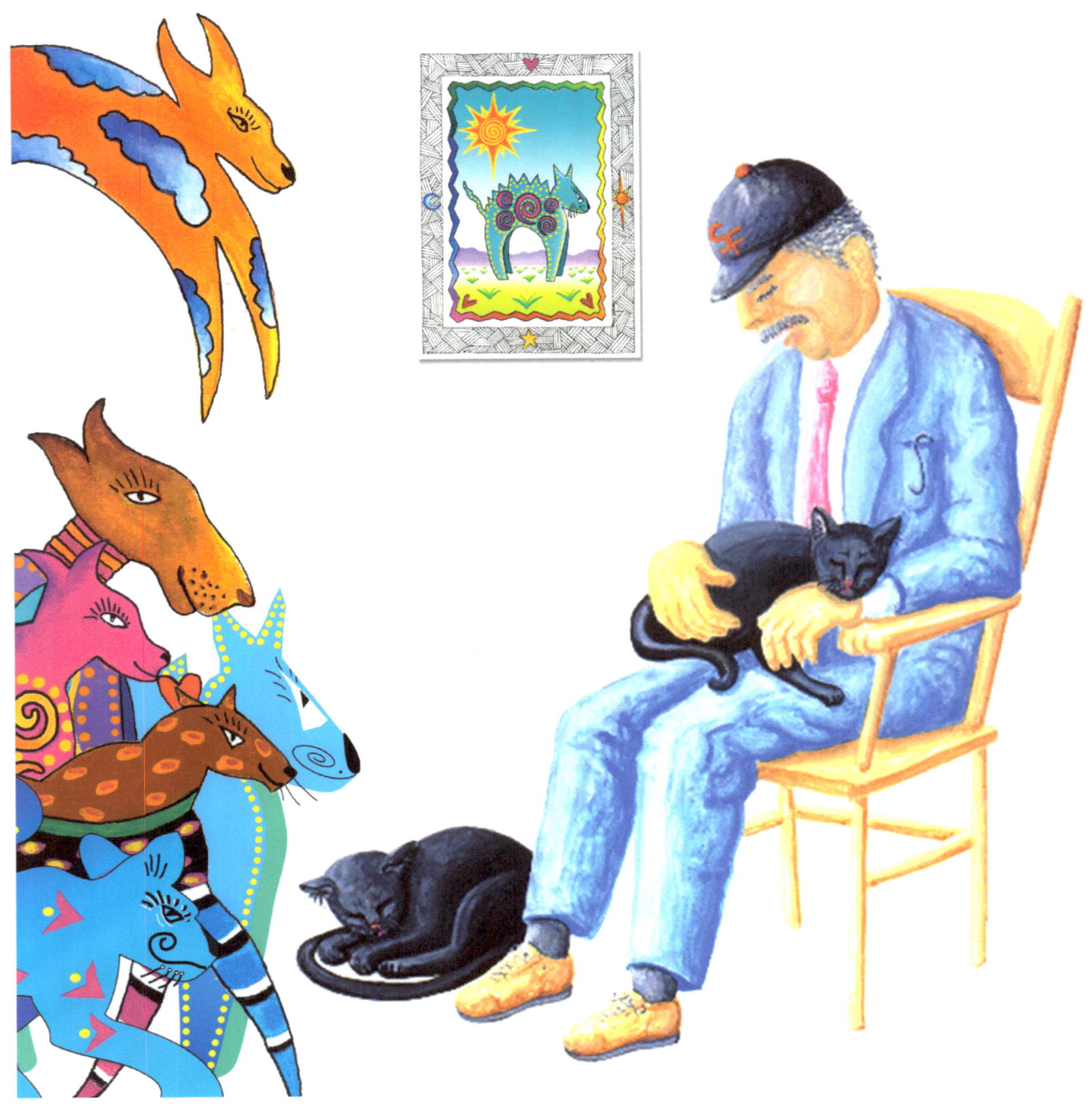

www.ingramcontent.com/pod-product-compliance
Lightning Source LLC
Chambersburg PA
CBHW050405180526

45159CB00005B/2160